William Ernest Henley

**London Voluntaries**

The Song of the Sword and other Verses

William Ernest Henley

**London Voluntaries**
*The Song of the Sword and other Verses*

ISBN/EAN: 9783744775427

Printed in Europe, USA, Canada, Australia, Japan

Cover: Foto ©Thomas Meinert / pixelio.de

More available books at **www.hansebooks.com**

# LONDON

# VOLUNTARIES

## THE SONG OF THE SWORD

## AND OTHER VERSES

BY

W. E. HENLEY

LONDON

Published by DAVID NUTT

in the Strand

1893

*Second Edition*

*Revised*

# To R. T. Hamilton-Bruce

*Edinburgh, Mar.* 17, 1892.

# CONTENTS

# CONTENTS

# CONTENTS

# LONDON

# VOLUNTARIES

## (To Charles Whibley)

*Andante con moto*

FORTH from the dust and din,

The crush, the heat, the many-spotted glare,

The odour and sense of life and lust aflare,

The wrangle and jangle of unrests,

Let us take horse, dear heart, take horse and
    win—

As from swart August to the green lap of May—

To quietness and the fresh and fragrant breasts

Of the still, delicious night, not yet aware

In any of her innumerable nests

Of that first sudden plash of dawn,

Clear, sapphirine, luminous, large,

Which tells that soon the flowing springs of day

3

In deep and ever deeper eddies drawn
Forward and up, in wider and wider way
Shall float the sands and brim the shores
On this our haunch of Earth, as round she roars
And spins into the outlook of the Sun
(The Lord's first gift, the Lord's especial charge),
With light, with living light, from marge to
    marge
Until the course He set and staked be run.


Through street and square, through square and
    street,
Each with his home-grown quality of dark
And violated silence, loud and fleet,
Waylaid by a merry ghost at every lamp,
The hansom wheels and plunges. Hark, O hark,
Sweet, how the old mare's bit and chain

Ring back a rough refrain
Upon the marked and cheerful tramp
Of her four shoes!  Here is the Park,
And O the languid midsummer wafts adust
The tired midsummer blooms!
O the mysterious distances, the glooms
Romantic, the august
And solemn shapes!  At night this City of
   Trees
Turns to a tryst of vague and strange
And monstrous Majesties,
Let loose from some dim underworld to range
These terrene vistas till their twilight sets:
When, dispossessed of wonderfulness, they stand
Beggared and common, plain to all the land
For stooks of leaves!  And lo! the wizard Hour
His silent, shining sorcery winged with power!
Still, still the streets, between their carcanets

Of linking gold, are avenues of sleep.

But see how gable ends and parapets

In gradual beauty and significance

Emerge! And did you hear

That little twitter-and-cheep,

Breaking inordinately loud and clear

On this still, spectral, exquisite atmosphere?

'Tis a first nest at matins! And behold

A rakehell cat—how furtive and acold!

A spent witch homing from some infamous
    dance—

Obscene, quick-trotting, see her tip and fade

Through shadowy railings into a pit of shade!

And now! a little wind and shy,

The smell of ships (that earnest of romance),

A sense of space and water, and thereby

A lamplit bridge ouching the troubled sky,

And look, O look! a tangle of silver gleams

And dusky lights, our River and all his dreams,
His dreams that never save in our deaths can die.

What miracle is happening in the air,
Charging the very texture of the gray
With something luminous and rare?
The night goes out like an ill-parcelled fire,
And, as one lights a candle, it is day.
The extinguisher that perks it like a spire
On the little formal church is not yet green
Across the water: but the house-tops nigher,
The corner-lines, the chimneys—look how clean,
How new, how naked! See the batch of boats,
Here at the stairs, washed in the fresh-sprung
    beam!
And those are barges that were goblin floats,
Black, hag-steered, fraught with devilry and dream!
And in the piles the water frolics clear,

7

The ripples into loose rings wander and flee,
And we—we can behold that could but hear
The ancient River singing as he goes
New-mailed in morning to the ancient Sea.
The gas burns lank and jaded in its glass :
The old Ruffian soon shall yawn himself awake,
And light his pipe, and shoulder his tools, and take
His hobnailed way to work !
                    Let us too pass :
Through these long blindfold rows
Of casements staring blind to right and left,
Each with his gaze turned inward on some piece
Of life in death's own likeness—Life bereft
Of living looks as by the Great Release
(Perchance of shadow-shapes from shadow-shows),
Whose upsnot all men know yet no man knows.


Reach upon reach of burial—so they feel,

These colonies of dreams !   And as we steal

Homeward together, but for the buxom breeze

Fitfully frolicking to heel

With news of dawn-drenched woods and tumbling
    seas,

We might — thus awed, thus lonely that we
    are—

Be wandering some depopulated star,

Some world of memories and unbroken graves,

So broods the abounding Silence near and far ·

Till even your footfall craves

Forgiveness of the majesty it braves.

# LONDON VOLUNTARIES

## II

*Scherzando*

Down through the ancient Strand
The Spirit of October, mild and boon
And sauntering, takes his way
This golden end of afternoon,
As though the corn stood yellow in all the land
And the ripe apples dropped to the harvest-moon.

Lo! the round sun, half down the western slope—
Seen as along an unglazed telescope—
Lingers and lolls, loth to be done with day:
Gifting the long, lean, lanky street
And its abounding confluences of being
With aspects generous and bland ;
Making a thousand harnesses to shine

As with new ore from some enchanted mine,

And every horse's coat so full of sheen

He looks new-tailored, and every 'bus feels clean,

And never a hansom but is worth the feeing ;

And every jeweller within the pale

Offers a real Arabian Night for sale ;

And even the roar

Of the strong streams of toil that pause and pour

Eastward and westward sounds suffused—

Seems as it were bemused

And blurred and like the speech

Of lazy seas on a lotus-eating beach—

With this enchanted lustrousness,

This mellow magic, that  as a man's caress

Brings back to some faded face beloved before

A heavenly shadow of the grace it wore

Ere the poor eyes were minded to beseech)

Old things transfigures, and you hail and bless

Their looks of long-lapsed loveliness once more.

Till Clement's, angular and cold and staid,

Glimmers in glamour's very stuffs arrayed;

And Bride's, her aëry, unsubstantial charm,

Through flight on flight of springing, soaring stone

Grown flushed and warm,

Laughs into life high-mooded and fresh-blown;

And the high majesty of Paul's

Uplifts a voice of living light, and calls—

Calls to his millions to behold and see

How goodly this his London Town can be!

For earth and sky and air

Are golden everywhere,

And golden with a gold so suave and fine

The looking on it lifts the heart like wine.

Trafalgar Square

(The fountains volleying golden glaze)

Gleams like an angel-market.  High aloft

Over his couchant Lions in a haze

Shimmering and bland and soft,

A dust of chrysoprase,

Our Sailor takes the golden gaze

Of the saluting sun, and flames superb

As once he flamed it on his ocean round.

The dingy dreariness of the picture-place,

Turned very nearly bright,

Takes on a luminous transiency of grace,

And shows no more a scandal to the ground.

The very blind man pottering on the kerb,

Among the posies and the ostrich feathers

And the rude voices touched with all the weathers

Of the long, varying year,

Shares in the universal alms of light.

The windows, with their fleeting, flickering fires,

The height and spread of frontage shining sheer,

The quiring signs, the rejoicing roofs and
    spires—
'Tis El Dorado—El Dorado plain,
The Golden City! And when a girl goes by,
Look! as she turns her glancing head,
A call of gold is floated from her ear!
Golden, all golden! In a golden glory,
Long lapsing down a golden coasted sky,
The day not dies but seems
Dispersed in wafts and drifts of gold, and shed
Upon a past of golden song and story
And memories of gold and golden dreams.

## III

*Largo e mesto*

OUT of the poisonous East,

Over a continent of blight,

Like a maleficent Influence released

From the most squalid cellarage of hell,

·The Wind-Fiend, the abominable—

The hangman wind that tortures temper and

    light—

Comes slouching, sullen and obscene,

Hard on the skirts of the embittered night :

And in a cloud unclean

Of excremental humours, roused to strife

By the operation of some ruinous change

Wherever his evil mandate run and range

Into a dire intensity of life,

# LONDON VOLUNTARIES

A craftsman at his bench, he settles down
To the grim job of throttling London Town.


And, by a jealous lightlessness beset
That might have oppressed the dragons of old
    time
Crunching and groping in the abysmal slime,
A cave of cut-throat thoughts and villainous
    dreams,
Hag-rid and crying with cold and dirt and wet,
The afflicted city, prone from mark to mark
In shameful occultation, seems
A nightmare labyrinthine, dim and drifting,
With wavering gulfs and antic heights and shifting
Rent in the stuff of a material dark
Wherein the lamplight, scattered and sick and pale,
Shows like the leper's living blotch of bale :
Uncoiling monstrous into street on street

Paven with perils, teeming with mischance,
Where man and beast go blindfold and in dread,
Working with oaths and threats and faltering feet
Somewhither in the hideousness ahead ;
Working through wicked airs and deadly dews
That make the laden robber grin askance
At the good places in his black romance,
And the poor, loitering harlot rather choose
Go pinched and pined to bed
Than lurk and shiver and curse her wretched way
From arch to arch, scouting some threepenny prey.


Forgot his dawns and far-flushed afterglows,
His green garlands and windy eyots forgot,
The old Father-River flows,
His watchfires cores of menace in the gloom,
As he came oozing from the Pit, and bore,
Sunk in his filthily transfigured sides,

Shoals of dishonoured dead to tumble and rot

In the squalor of the universal shore :

His voices sounding through the gruesome air

As from the ferry where the Boat of Doom

With her blaspheming cargo reels and rides :

The while his children, the brave ships,

No more adventurous and fair,

Nor tripping it light of heel as home-bound
　　　brides,

But infamously enchanted,

Huddle together in the foul eclipse,

Or feel their course by inches desperately,

As through a tangle of alleys murder-haunted,

From sinister reach to reach out—out—to sea.


And Death the while—

Death with his well-worn, lean, professional smile,

Death in his threadbare working trim—

Comes to your bedside, unannounced and bland,

And with expert, inevitable hand

Feels at your windpipe, fingers you in the lung,

Or flicks the clot well into the labouring heart :

Thus signifying unto old and young,

However hard of mouth or wild of whim,

'Tis time—'tis time by his ancient watch—to part

With books and women and talk and drink and

    art :

And you go humbly after him

To a mean suburban lodging : on the way

To what or where

Not Death, who is old and very wise, can say :

And you—how should you care

So long as, unreclaimed of hell,

The Wind-Fiend, the insufferable,

Thus vicious and thus patient sits him down

To the black job of burking London Town ?

## IV

*Allegro maëstoso*

SPRING winds that blow
As over leagues of myrtle-blooms and may;
Bevies of spring clouds trooping slow,
Like matrons heavy-bosomed and aglow
With the mild and placid pride of increase!   Nay,
What makes this insolent and comely stream
Of appetence, this freshet of desire
(Milk from the wild breasts of the wilful Day!),
Down Piccadilly dance and murmur and gleam
In genial wave on wave and gyre on gyre?
Why does that nymph unparalleled splash and
     churn
The wealth of her enchanted urn
Till, over-billowing all between

Her cheerful margents grey and living green,

It floats and wanders, glittering and fleeing,

An estuary of the joy of being?

Why should the buxom leafage of the Park

Touch to an ecstasy the act of seeing?

—Sure, sure my paramour, my bride of brides,

Lingering and flushed, mysteriously abides

In some dim, eye-proof angle of odorous dark,

Some smiling nook of green-and-golden shade.

In the divine conviction robed and crowned

The globe fulfils his immemorial round

But as the marrying-place of all things made!


There is no man, this deifying day,

But feels the primal blessing in his blood.

The sacred impulse of the May

Brightening like sex made sunshine through her
   veins,

There is no woman but disdains

To vail the ensigns of her womanhood.

None but, rejoicing, flaunts them as she goes,

Bounteous in looks of her delicious best,

On her inviolable quest :

These with their hopes, with their sweet secrets

      those,

But all desirable and frankly fair,

As each were keeping some most prosperous tryst,

And in the knowledge went imparadised.

For look ! a magical influence everywhere,

Look how the liberal and transfiguring air

Washes this inn of memorable meetings,

This centre of ravishments and gracious greetings,

Till, through its jocund loveliness of length

A tidal-race of lust from shore to shore,

A brimming reach of beauty met with strength,

It shines and sounds like some miraculous dream,

Some vision multitudinous and agleam,
Of happiness as it shall be evermore !


Praise God for giving
Through this His messenger among the days
His word the life He gave is thrice-worth living !
For Pan, the bountiful, imperious Pan—
Not dead, not dead, as dreamers feigned,
But the gay genius of a million Mays
Renewing his beneficent endeavour !—
Still reigns and triumphs, as he hath triumphed
  and reigned
Since in the dim blue dawn of time
The universal ebb-and-flow began,
To sound his ancient music, and prevails
By the persuasion of his mighty rhyme
Here in this radiant and immortal street
Lavishly and omnipotently as ever

In the open hills, the undissembling dales,
The laughing-places of the juvenile earth.
For lo ! the wills of man and woman meet,
Meet and are moved, each unto each endeared
As once in Eden's prodigal bowers befell,
To share his shameless, elemental mirth
In one great act of faith, while deep and strong,
Incomparably nerved and cheered,
The enormous heart of London joys to beat
To the measures of his rough, majestic song :
The lewd, perennial, overmastering spell
That keeps the rolling universe ensphered
And life and all for which life lives to long
Wanton and wondrous and for ever well.

# THE SONG
# OF THE SWORD

(To Rudyard Kipling)

*The Sword*

*Singing—*

*The voice of the Sword from the heart*

   *of the Sword*

*Clanging imperious*

*Forth from Time's battlements*

*His ancient and triumphing Song.*


In the beginning,

Ere God inspired Himself

Into the clay thing

Thumbed to His image,

The vacant, the naked shell

Soon to be Man:

27

Thoughtful He pondered it,
Prone there and impotent,
Fragile, inviting
Attack and discomfiture :
Then, with a smile—
As He heard in the Thunder
That laughed over Eden
The voice of the Trumpet,
The iron Beneficence,
Calling His dooms
To the Winds of the world—
Stooping, He drew
On the sand with His finger
A shape for a sign
Of His way to the eyes
That in wonder should waken,
For a proof of His will
To the breaking intelligence :

# THE SWORD

That was the birth of me:
I am the Sword.

Bleak and lean, gray and cruel,
Short-hilted, long-shafted,
I froze into steel:
And the blood of my elder,
His hand on the hafts of me,
Sprang like a wave
In the wind, as the sense
Of his strength grew to ecstasy;
Glowed like a coal
In the throat of the furnace,
As he knew me and named me
The War-Thing, the Comrade,
Father of honour
And giver of kingship,
The fame-smith, the song-master,

## THE SONG OF

Bringer of women
On fire at his hands
For the pride of fulfilment,
*Priest* (saith the Lord)
*Of his marriage with victory.*
Ho! then, the Trumpet,
Handmaid of heroes,
Calling the peers
To the place of espousals!
Ho! then, the splendour
And sheen of my ministry,
Clothing the earth
With a livery of lightnings :
Ho! then, the music
Of battles in onset
And ruining armours
And God's gift returning
In fury to God!

# THE SWORD

Thrilling and keen
As the song of the winter stars,
Ho! then, the sound
Of my voice, the implacable
Angel of Destiny!—
I am the Sword.


Heroes, my children,
Follow, O follow me,
Follow, exulting
In the great light that breaks
From the sacred Companionship:
Thrust through the fatuous,
Thrust through the fungous brood
Spawned in my shadow
And gross with my gift!
Thrust through, and hearken,
O hark, to the Trumpet,

The Virgin of Battles,
Calling, still calling you
Into the Presence,
Sons of the Judgment,
Pure wafts of the Will!
Edged to annihilate,
Hilted with government,
Follow, O follow me
Till the waste places
All the gray globe over
Ooze, as the honeycomb
Drips, with the sweetness
Distilled of my strength:
And, teeming in peace
Through the wrath of my coming,
They give back in beauty
The dread and the anguish
They had of me visitant!

# THE SWORD

Follow, O follow, then,
Heroes, my harvesters!
Where the tall grain is ripe
Thrust in your sickles:
Stripped and adust
In a stubble of empire,
Scything and binding
The full sheaves of sovranty:
Thus, O thus gloriously,
Shall you fulfil yourselves:
Thus, O thus mightily,
Show yourselves sons of mine—
Yea, and win grace of me:
I am the Sword.

I am the feast-maker:
Hark, through a noise
Of the screaming of eagles,

Hark how the Trumpet,
The mistress of mistresses,
Calls, silver-throated
And stern, where the tables
Are spread, and the work
Of the Lord is in hand!
Driving the darkness,
Even as the banners
And spears of the Morning;
Sifting the nations,
The slag from the metal,
The waste and the weak
From the fit and the strong;
Fighting the brute,
The abysmal Fecundity;
Checking the gross,
Multitudinous blunders,
The groping, the purblind

# THE SWORD

Excesses in service
Of the Womb universal,
The absolute Drudge;
Changing the charactry
Carved on the World,
The miraculous gem
In the seal-ring that burns
On the hand of the Master—
Yea! and authority
Flames through the dim,
Unappeasable Grisliness
Prone down the nethermost
Chasms of the Void;
Clear singing, clean slicing;
Sweet spoken, soft finishing;
Making death beautiful,
Life but a coin
To be staked in the pastime

## THE SONG OF THE SWORD

Whose playing is more
Than the transfer of being;
Arch-anarch, chief builder,
Prince and evangelist,
I am the Will of God:
I am the Sword.

*The Sword*
*Singing—*
*The voice of the Sword from the heart*
*of the Sword*
*Clanging majestical.*
*As from the starry-staired*
*Courts of the primal Supremacy,*
*His high, irresistible song.*

# ARABIAN NIGHTS'
# ENTERTAINMENTS

(To Elizabeth Robins Pennell)

ONCE on a time
There was a little boy : a master-mage
By virtue of a Book
Of magic—O so magical it filled
His life with visionary pomps
Processional !   And Powers
Passed with him where he passed.   And Thrones
And Dominations, glaived and plumed and mailed,
Thronged in the criss-cross streets,
The palaces pell-mell with playing-fields,
Domes, cloisters, dungeons, caverns, tents, arcades,
Of the unseen, silent City, in his soul
Pavilioned jealously and hid

As in the dusk, profound,
Green stillnesses of some enchanted mere.— — —


I shut mine eyes. . . . And lo!
A flickering snatch of memory that floats
Upon the face of a pool of darkness five
And thirty dead years deep,
Antic in girlish broideries
And skirts and silly shoes with straps
And a broad-ribanded leghorn, he walks
Plain in the shadow of a church
(St. Michael's : in whose brazen call
To curfew his first wails of wrath were whelmed)
Sedate for all his haste
To be at home; and, nestled in his arm,
Inciting still to quiet and solitude,
Boarded in sober drab,
With small, square, agitating cuts

# ENTERTAINMENTS

Let in atop of the double-columned, close,

Quakerlike print, a Book ! . . .

What but that blessèd brief

Of what is gallantest and best

In all the full-shelved Libraries of Romance ?

The Book of rocs,

Sandalwood, ivory, turbans, ambergris,

Cream-tarts, and lettered apes, and calenders,

And ghouls, and genies—O so huge

They might have overed the tall Minster

    Tower

Hands down, as schoolboys take a post !

In truth, the Book of Camaralzaman,

Schemselnihar and Sindbad, Scheherezade

The peerless, Bedreddin, Badroulbadour,

Cairo and Serendib and Candahar,

And Caspian, and the haunted bulk —

Ice-ribbed, tremendous, inaccessible—

Of Kaf! . . . That centre of miracles,
The sole, unparalleled Arabian Nights!

Old friends I had a-many—kindly and grim
Familiars, cronies quaint
And goblin! Never a Wood but housed
Some morrice of dainty dapperlings: no Brook
But had his nunnery
Of green-haired, silvry-curving sprites
To cabin in his grots and pace
His lilied margents: every lone hillside
Might open upon Elf-Land: every Stalk
That curled about a Beanstick was of the breed
Of that live ladder by whose delicate rungs
You climbed beyond the clouds, and found
The Farm-House where the Ogre, gorged
And drowsy, from his great oak chair,
Among the flitches and pewters at the fire,

# ENTERTAINMENTS

Called for his Faëry Harp that came
And, perching on the kitchen table, sang
Jocund and jubilant, with a sound
Of those gay, golden-vowelled madrigals
The shy thrush at mid-May
Flutes from wet orchards flushed with the
    triumphing dawn,
With blackbirds rioting as they listened still
In old-world woodlands rapt with an old-world
    spring
For Pan's own whistle, savage and rich and lewd,
And mocked him call for call.
                I could not pass
The half-door where the cobbler sat in view
Nor figure me the wizen Leprechaun
In square-cut, faded reds and buckle-shoes
Bent at his work in the hedge-side, and know
Just how he tapped his brogue, and twitched

His wax-end this and that way, both with wrists
And elbows.   In the rich June fields,
Where the ripe clover drew the bees,
And the tall quakers trembled, and the West
   Wind
Lolled his half-holiday away beside
Me idling down my own,
"Twas good to follow the Miller's Youngest
   Son
On his white horse along the leafy lanes ;
For at his stirrup linked and ran,
Not cynical and trapesing, as he lounged
From wall to wall above the espaliers,
But in the bravest tops
That market-town, a town of tops, could show,
Bold, subtle, adventurous, his tail
A banner flaunted in disdain
Of human stratagems and shifts,

# ENTERTAINMENTS

King over All the Catlands, present and past
And future, that moustached
Artificer of fortunes, Puss in Boots.
Or Bluebeard's Closet, with its plenishing
Of meat-hooks, sawdust, blood,
And wives that hung like fresh-dressed carcases—
Odd-fangled, most a butcher's, part
A faëry chamber hazily seen
And hazily figured—on dark afternoons
And windy nights was visiting of the best.
Then, too, the pelt of hoofs
Out in the roaring darkness told
Of Herne the Hunter in his antlered helm
Galloping as with despatches from the Pit
Between his hell-born Hounds.
And Rip Van Winkle . . . often I lurked to hear
Outside the long, low timbered wall,
The mutter and rumble of the trolling bowls

45

Down the lean plank before they fluttered the
    pins :
For, listening so, myself could help him play
His wonderful game
With Hendrik Hudson deep in those haunted
    hills.

But what were these so near,
So neighbourly fancies to the spell that brought
The run of Ali Baba's Cave
Just for the saying 'Open Sesame,'
With gold to measure, peck by peck,
In round, brown wooden stoups
You borrowed at the chandler's? . . . Or one
    time
Made you Aladdin's friend at school
Free of his Garden of Jewels, Ring and Lamp
In perfect trim? . . . Or Ladies fair,

But their white bosoms seamed with embrown-
   ing scars,
Went labouring under some dread ordinance
Which made them whip, and bitterly cry the
   while,
Strange Curs that wept as they,
Till there was never a Black Bitch of all
Your consorting but might have gone
Spell-driven miserably for crimes
Done in the pride of womanhood and desire . . .
Or at the ghostliest altitudes of night,
While you lay wondering and acold,
Your sense was fearfully purged, and soon
Queen Labe, abominable and dear,
Rose from your side, opened the Box of Doom,
Scattered the yellow powder (which I saw
Like sulphur at the Docks in bulk)
And muttered certain words you could not hear:

47

And there ! a living stream,
The brook you bathed in, with its weeds and flags
And cresses, glittered and sang
Out of the hearthrug over the nakedness
Well-scrubbed and decent of your bedroom
    floor ! . . .

I was—how many a time !—
That Second Calender, Son of a King,
On whom 'twas vehemently enjoined,
Pausing at one mysterious door,
To pry no closer but content his soul
With his kind Forty.   Yet I could not rest
For idleness and ungovernable Fate.
And the Black Horse, who fed on sesame
(That wonder-working word !),
Took me upon his back, and spread his vans,
And soaring, soaring on

# ENTERTAINMENTS

From air to air, came charging to the ground
Sheer, like a lark from the midsummer clouds,
And, shaking me out of the saddle, where I
    sprawled
Flicked at me with his tail
And left me blinded, miserable, distraught
(Even as I was in deed
When doctors came and odious things were done
On my poor tortured eyes
With lancets, or some evil acid stung
And wrung them like hot sand,
And desperately from room to room
Fumble I must my dark, disconsolate way)
To get to Bagdad how I might.   But there
I met with Merry Ladies.   O you three—
Safie, Amine, Zobeïde—when my heart
Forgets you all shall be forgot !
And so we supped, we and the rest,

On wine and roasted lamb, rose-water, dates,

Almonds, pistachios, citrons.　And Haroun

Laughed out of his lordly beard

On Giaffar and Mesrour (I knew the Three

For all their Mossoul habits !).　And outside

The Tigris, flowing swift

Like Severn bend for bend, twinkled and gleamed

With broken and wavering shapes of stranger
　　　stars :

The vast blue night

Was murmurous with peris' plumes

And the leathern wings of genies : words of
　　　power

Were whispering : and old fishermen,

Casting their nets with prayer, might draw to
　　　shore

Dead loveliness ; or a prodigy in scales

Worth in the Caliph's Kitchen pieces of gold ;

# ENTERTAINMENTS

Or copper vessels stopped with lead
Wherein some Squire of Eblis watched and railed,
In durance under the potent charactry
Graved by the seal of Solomon the King. . . .

Then, as the Book was glassed
In Life as in some olden mirror's quaint,
Bewildering angles, so would Life
Flash light on light back on the Book : and both
Were changed.  Once in a house decayed
From better days, harbouring an errant show
(For all its stories of dry-rot
Were filled with gruesome visitants in wax,
Inhuman, hushed, ghastly with Painted Eyes),
I wandered ; and no living soul
Was nearer than the pay-box ; and I stared
Upon them staring—staring.  Till at last,
Three sets of rafters from the streets,

I strayed upon a mildewed, rat-run room
With the two Dancers, horrible and obscene,
Guarding the door: and there, in a bedroom-set,
Behind a fence of faded crimson cords,
With an aspect of frills
And dimities and dishonoured privacy
That made you hanker and hesitate to look,
A Woman with her litter of Babes—all slain,
All in their nightgowns, all with Painted Eyes
Staring—still staring; so that I turned and ran
As for my neck.   The same, it seemed,
And yet not all the same, I was to find,
As I went up.   For afterward
Whenas I went my round alone—
All day alone—in long, stern, silent streets,
Where I might stretch my hand and take
Whatever I would: still there were Shapes of
    Stone,

Motionless, lifelike, frightening—for the Wrath
Had smitten them; but they watched,
This by her melons and figs, that by his rings
And chains and watches, with the hideous gaze,
The Painted Eyes insufferable,
Now, of those grisly images; and I
Pursued my best-beloved quest
Thrilled with a novel and delicious fear.
So the night fell—with never a lamplighter;
And through the Palace of the King
I groped among the echoes, and I felt
That they were there,
Dreadfully there, the Painted staring Eyes,
Hall after hall . . . Till lo! from far
A Voice! And in a little while
Two tapers burning! And the Voice
Heard in the wondrous Word of God was—whose?
Whose but Zobeïde's,

53

The lady of my heart, like me
A True Believer, and like me
An outcast leagues and leagues beyond the
    pale! . . .


Or, sailing to the Isles
Of Khaledan, I spied one evenfall
A black blotch in the sunset; and it grew
Swiftly . . . and grew.   Tearing their beards,
The sailors wept and prayed; but the grave ship,
Deep-laden with spiceries and pearls, went mad,
Wrenched the long tiller out of the steersman's
    hand,
And, turning broadside on,
As the most iron would, was haled and sucked
Nearer, and nearer yet;
And, all awash, with horrible lurching leaps
Rushed at that Portent, casting a shadow now

# ENTERTAINMENTS

That swallowed sea and sky ; and then
Anchors and nails and bolts
Flew screaming out of her, and with clang on
    clang,
A noise of fifty stithies, caught at the sides
Of the Magnetic Mountain ; and she lay,
A broken bundle of firewood, strown piecemeal
About the waters ; and her crew
Passed shrieking, one by one ; and I was left
To drown. All the long night I swam ;
But in the morning, O the smiling coast
Tufted with date-trees, meadowlike,
Skirted with shelving sands ! And a great
    wave
Cast me ashore ; and I was saved alive.
But, giving thanks to God, I dried my clothes,
And, faring inland, in a desert place
I stumbled on an iron ring—

The fellow of fifty built into the Quays :
When, scenting a trap-door,
I dug, and dug ; until my biggest blade
Stuck into wood.   And then,
The flight of smooth-hewn, easygoing stairs
Sunk in the naked rock !   The cool, clean vault,
So neat with niche on niche it might have been
Our beer-cellar but for the rows
Of brazen urns (like monstrous chemist's jars)
Full to the wide, squat throats
With gold-dust, but atop
A layer of pickled-walnut-looking things
I knew for olives !   And far, O far away,
The Princess of China languished !   Far away
Was marriage, with a Vizier and a Chief
Of Eunuchs and the privilege
Of going out at night
To play—unkenned, majestical, secure—

# ENTERTAINMENTS

Where the old, brown, friendly river shaped
Like Tigris shore for shore!  Haply a Ghoul
Sat in the churchyard under a frightened moon,
A thighbone in his fist, and glared
At supper with a Lady: she who took
Her rice with tweezers grain by grain.
Or you might stumble, there by the iron gates—
Of the Pump Room—underneath the limes
Upon Bedreddin in his shirt and drawers,
Just as the civil Genie laid him down.
Or those red-curtained panes,
Whence a tame cornet tenored it throatily
Of beer-pots and spittoons and new long pipes
Might turn a caravansery's, wherein
You found Noureddin Ali, loftily drunk,
And that Fair Persian, bathed in tears,
You 'd not have given away
For all the diamonds in the Vale Perilous

You had that dark and disleaved afternoon
Escaped on a roc's claw,
Disguised like Sindbad—but in Christmas beef!
And all the blissful while
The schoolboy satchel at your hip
Was such a bulse of gems as should amaze
Gray-whiskered chapmen drawn
From over Caspian : yea, the Chief Jewellers
Of Tartary and the bazaars,
Seething with traffic, of enormous Ind !— — —


Thus cried, thus called aloud, to the child heart
The magian East : thus the child eyes
Spelled out the wizard message by the light
Of the sober workaday hours
They saw, week in week out, pass, and still pass
In the sleepy Minster City folded kind
In ancient Severn's arm,

# ENTERTAINMENTS

Amongst her water-meadows and her docks

Whose floating populace of ships—

Galliots and luggers, light-heeled brigantines,

Bluff barques and rake-hell fore-and-afters—
  brought

To her very doorsteps and geraniums

The scents of the World's End, the calls

That may not be gainsaid to rise and ride

Like fire on some high errand of the race,

The irresistible appeals

For comradeship that sound

Steadily from the irresistible sea.

Thus the East laughed and whispered, and the
  tale,

Telling itself anew

In terms of living labouring life,

Took on the colours, busked it in the wear,

Of life that lived and laboured : and Romance,

The Angel-Playmate, raining down

His golden influences

On all I saw, and all I dreamed and did,

Walked with me arm and arm,

Or left me, as one bediademed with straws

And bits of glass, to gladden at my heart

Who had the gift to seek and feel and find

His fiery-hearted presence everywhere.

Even as dear Hesper, bringer of all good things,

Sends the same silver dews

Of happiness down her dim, delighted skies

On some poor collier-hamlet—(mound on mound

Of sifted squalor; here a soot-throated stalk

Sullenly smoking over a row

Of flat-faced hovels; black in the gritty air

A web of rails and wheels and beams; with

    strings

Of hurtling, tipping trams)—

# ENTERTAINMENTS

As on the amorous nightingales
And roses of Shiraz or the walls and towers
Of Samarcand—the Ineffable—whence you espy
The splendour of Ginnistan's embattled spears
Like listed summer lightnings.

Samarcand !
That name of names !   That star-vaned belvedere
Builded against the Chambers of the South !
That outpost on the Infinite !

And, behold !
Questing therefrom, you knew not what wild tide
Might overtake you :  for one fringe,
One suburb, is stablished on firm earth ;  but one
Floats founded vague
In lubberlands delectable—isles of palm
And lotus, fortunate mains, far-shimmering seas,
The promise of wistful hills—
The shining, shifting Sovranties of Dream.

# RHYMES
## AND RHYTHMS

63

WHERE forlorn sunsets flare and fade
  On desolate sea and lonely sand,
Out of the silence and the shade
  What is the voice of strange command
Calling you still, as friend calls friend
  With love that cannot brook delay,
To rise and follow the ways that wend
  Over the hills and far away?

Hark in the city, street on street
  A roaring reach of death and life,
Of vortices that clash and fleet
  And ruin in appointed strife,

E                    65

Hark to it calling, calling clear,
Calling until you cannot stay
From dearer things than your own most dear
Over the hills and far away.

Out of the sound of ebb and flow,
Out of the sight of lamp and star,
It calls you where the good winds blow,
And the unchanging meadows are:
From faded hopes and hopes agleam,
It calls you, calls you night and day
Beyond the dark into the dream
Over the hills and far away.

II

(To R. F. B.)

WE are the Choice of the Will: God, when He
gave the word
That called us into line, set in our hand a sword;

Set us a sword to wield none else could lift and
draw,
And bade us forth to the sound of the trumpet
of the Law.

East and west and north, wherever the battle
grew,
As men to a feast we fared, the work of the
Will to do.

Bent upon vast beginnings, bidding anarchy
cease—

(Had we hacked it to the Pit, we had left it a
place of peace!)—

Marching, building, sailing, pillar of cloud or fire,
Sons of the Will, we fought the fight of the Will,
our sire.

Road was never so rough that we left its purpose
dark;
Stark was ever the sea, but our ships were yet
more stark;

We tracked the winds of the world to the steps
of their very thrones;
The secret parts of the world were salted with
our bones;

Till now the name of names, England, the name
of might,
Flames from the austral bounds to the ends of
the boreal night;

And the call of her morning drum goes in a
girdle of sound,
Like the voice of the sun in song, the great
globe round and round;

And the shadow of her flag, when it shouts to the
mother-breeze,
Floats from shore to shore of the universal seas;

And the loneliest death is fair with a memory of
her flowers,
And the end of the road to Hell with the sense
of her dews and showers!

69

Who says that we shall pass, or the fame of us
  fade and die,
While the living stars fulfil their round in the
  living sky?

For the sire lives in his sons, and they pay their
  father's debt,
And the Lion has left a whelp wherever his claw
  was set:

And the Lion in his whelps, his whelps that
  none shall brave,
Is but less strong than Time and the great, all-
  whelming Grave.·

III

A DESOLATE shore,
The sinister seduction of the Moon,
The menace of the irreclaimable Sea.

Flaunting, tawdry and grim,
From cloud to cloud along her beat,
Leering her battered and inveterate leer,
She signals where he prowls in the dark alone,
Her horrible old man,
Mumbling old oaths and warming
His villainous old bones with villainous talk—
The secrets of their grisly housekeeping
Since they went out upon the pad

In the first twilight of self-conscious Time :
Growling, hideous and hoarse,
Tales of unnumbered Ships,
Goodly and strong, Companions of the Advance
In some vile alley of the night
Waylaid and bludgeoned—
Dead.


Deep cellared in primeval ooze,
Ruined, dishonoured, spoiled,
They lie where the lean water-worm
Crawls free of their secrets, and their broken
    sides
Bulge with the slime of life.  Thus they abide,
Thus fouled and desecrate,
The summons of the Trumpet, and the while
These Twain, their murderers,
Unravined, imperturbable unsubdued,

Hang at the heels of their children—She aloft

As in the shining streets,

He as in ambush by some fetid stair.


The stalwart Ships,

The beautiful and bold adventurers !

Stationed out yonder in the isle,

The tall Policeman,

Flashing his bull's-eye, as he peers

About him in the ancient vacancy,

Tells them this way is safety—this way home.

IV

It came with the threat of a waning moon
   And the wail of an ebbing tide,
But many a woman has lived for less,
   And many a man has died ;
For life upon life took hold and passed,
   Strong in a fate set free,
Out of the deep into the dark
   On for the years to be.


Between the gleam of a waning moon
   And the song of an ebbing tide,
Chance upon chance of love and death
   Took wing for the world so wide.

74

Leaf out of leaf is the way of the land,
  Wave out of wave of the sea
And who shall reckon what lives may live
  In the life that we bade to be?

## V

Why, my heart, do we love her so?
  (Geraldine, Geraldine!)—
Why does the great sea ebb and flow?
  Why does the round world spin?
Geraldine, Geraldine,
  Bid me my life renew,
What is it worth unless I win,
  Love—love and you?

Why, my heart, when we speak her name
  (Geraldine, Geraldine!),
Throbs the word like a flinging flame?—
  Why does the Spring begin?

Geraldine, Geraldine,
  Bid me indeed to be,
Open your heart and take us in,
  Love—love and me.

## VI

One with the ruined sunset,
  The strange forsaken sands,
What is it waits and wanders
  And signs with desperate hands?

What is it calls in the twilight—
  Calls as its chance were vain?
The cry of a gull sent seaward
  Or the voice of an ancient pain?

The red ghost of the sunset,
  It walks them as its own,
These dreary and desolate reaches . . .
  But O that it walked alone!

## VII

THERE's a regret
So grinding, so immitigably sad,
Remorse thereby feels tolerant, even glad. . . .
Do you not know it yet?

For deeds undone
Rankle and snarl and hunger for their due
Till there seems naught so despicable as you
In all the grin o' the sun.

Like an old shoe
The sea spurns and the land abhors, you lie
About the beach of Time, till by-and-by
Death, that derides you too—

Death, as he goes
His ragman's round, espies you where you stray
With half-an-eye, and kicks you out of his way ;
And then—and then, who knows

But the kind Grave
Turns on you, and you feel the convict Worm,
In that black bridewell working out his term,
Hanker and grope and crave ?

' Poor fool that might—
That might, yet would not, dared not, let this be,
Think of it, here and thus made over to me
In the implacable night ! '

And writhing, fain
And like a triumphing lover, he shall take
His fill where no high memory lives to make
His obscene victory vain.

## VIII

### (To A. J. H.)

TIME and the Earth—
The old Father and Mother—
Their teeming accomplished,
Their purpose fulfilled,
Close with a smile
For a moment of kindness
Ere for the winter
They settle to sleep.

Failing yet gracious,
Slow pacing, soon homing,
A patriarch that strolls
Through the tents of his children,
The Sun, as he journeys
His round on the lower

Ascents of the blue,
Washes the roofs
And the hillsides with clarity;
Charms the dark pools
Till they break into pictures;
Scatters magnificent
Alms to the beggar trees;
Touches the mist-folk
That crowd to his escort
Into translucencies
Radiant and ravishing,
As with the visible
Spirit of Summer
Gloriously vaporised,
Visioned in gold.

Love, though the fallen leaf
Mark, and the fleeting light

And the loud, loitering
Footfall of darkness
Sign to the heart
Of the passage of destiny,
Here is the ghost
Of a summer that lived for us,
Here is a promise
Of summers to be.

IX

'As like the Woman as you can '—

(*Thus the New Adam was beguiled*) —

'So shall you touch the Perfect Man '—

(*God in the Garden heard and smiled*).

'Your father perished with his day :

'A clot of passions fierce and blind

'He fought, he hacked, he crushed his way :

'Your muscles, Child, must be of mind.


'The Brute that lurks and irks within,

'How, till you have him gagged and bound,

'Escape the foullest form of Sin ? '

(*God in the Garden laughed and frowned*).

84

'So vile, so rank, the bestial mood
  'In which the race is bid to be,
' It wrecks the Rarer Womanhood :
  ' Live, therefore, you, for Purity!


' Take for your mate no gallant croup,
  ' No girl all grace and natural will :
' To work her mission were to stoop
  ' Maybe to lapse, from Well to Ill.
' Choose one of whom your grosser make '—
  (God in the Garden laughed outright)—
' The true refining touch may take
  ' Till both attain to Life's last height.


' There, equal, purged of soul and sense,
  ' Beneficent, high-thinking, just,
' Beyond the appeal of Violence,
  ' Incapable of common Lust,

85

'In mental Marriage still prevail'—

(*God in the Garden hid His face*)—

'Till you achieve that Female-Male

   'In Which shall culminate the race'.

X

Midsummer midnight skies,
Midsummer midnight influences and airs,
The shining sensitive silver of the sea
Touched with the strange-hued blazonings of dawn :
And all so solemnly still I seem to hear
The breathing of Life and Death,
The secular Accomplices,
Renewing the visible miracle of the world.


The wistful stars
Shine like good memories.   The young morning
    wind
Blows full of unforgotten hours

87

As over a region of roses.   Life and Death

Sound on—sound on. . . . And the night magical,

Troubled yet comforting, thrills

As if the Enchanted Castle at the heart

Of the wood's dark wonderment

Swung wide his valves  and filled the dim sea
  banks

With exquisite visitants :

Words fiery-hearted yet, dreams and desires

With living looks intolerable, regrets

Whose voice comes as the voice of an only child

Heard from the grave : shapes of a Might-Have-
  Been—

Beautiful, miserable, distraught—

The Law no man may baffle denied and slew.


The spell-bound ships stand as at gaze

To let the marvel by.  The grey road glooms . . .

Glimmers . . . goes out . . . and there, O there
    where it fades,
What grace, what glamour, what wild will,
Transfigure the shadows? Whose,
Heart of my heart, Soul of my soul, but yours?


Ghosts—ghosts—the sapphirine air
Teems with them even to the gleaming ends
Of the wild day-spring! Ghosts,
Everywhere—everywhere—till I and you
At last—dear love, at last!—
Are in the dreaming, even as Life and Death,
Twin-ministers of the unoriginal Will.

## XI

GULLS in an aëry morrice
  Gleam and vanish and gleam . . .
The full sea, sleepily basking,
  Dreams under skies of dream.

Gulls in an aëry morrice
  Circle and swoop and close . . .
Fuller and ever fuller
  The rose of the morning blows.

Gulls in an aëry morrice
  Frolicking float and fade . . .
O the way of a bird in the sunshine,
  The way of a man with a maid !

## XII

Some starlit garden grey with dew,
Some chamber flushed with wine and fire,
What matters where, so I and you
    Are worthy our desire ?

Behind, a past that scolds and jeers
For ungirt loin and lamp unlit ;
In front the unmanageable years,
    The trap upon the Pit ;

Think on the shame of dreams for deeds,
The scandal of unnatural strife,
The slur upon immortal needs,
    The treason done to life :

91

## RHYMES AND RHYTHMS

Arise! no more a living lie
And with me quicken and control
A memory that shall magnify
The universal Soul.

# RHYMES AND RHYTHMS

## XIII

(To James McNeill Whistler)

UNDER a stagnant sky,
Gloom out of gloom uncoiling into gloom,
The River, jaded and forlorn,
Welters and wanders wearily—wretchedly—on ;
Yet in and out among the ribs
Of the old skeleton bridge, as in the piles
Of some dead lake-built city, full of skulls,
Worm-worn, rat-riddled, mouldy with memories,
Lingers to babble, to a broken tune
(Once, O the unvoiced music of my heart !)
So melancholy a soliloquy
It sounds as it might tell
The secret of the unending grief-in-grain,

The terror of Time and Change and Death,
That wastes this floating, transitory world.

What of the incantation
That forced the huddled shapes on yonder shore
To take and wear the night
Like a material majesty?
That touched the shafts of wavering fire
About this miserable welter and wash—
(River, O River of Journeys, River of Dreams!)—
Into long, shining signals from the panes
Of an enchanted pleasure-house
Where life and life might live life lost in life
For ever and evermore?

O Death! O Change! O Time!
Without you, O the insufferable eyes
Of these poor Might-Have-Beens,
These fatuous, ineffectual Yesterdays!

.

XIV

(To J. A. C.)

Fresh from his fastnesses
Wholesome and spacious,
The north wind, the mad huntsman,
Halloos on his white hounds
Over the grey, roaring
Reaches and ridges,
The forest of ocean,
The chace of the world.

Hark to the peal
Of the pack in full cry,
As he thongs them before him
Swarming voluminous,
Weltering, wide-wallowing,

95

Till in a ruining
Chaos of energy,
Hurled on their quarry,
They crash into foam !

Old Indefatigable,
Time's right-hand man, the sea
Laughs as in joy
From his millions of wrinkles :
Laughs that his destiny,
Great with the greatness
Of triumphing order,
Shows as a dwarf
By the strength of his heart
And the might of his hands.

Master of masters,
O maker of heroes,

Thunder the brave,

Irresistible message :—

' Life is worth living

Through every grain of it

From the foundations

To the last edge

Of the cornerstone, death.'

## XV

You played and sang a snatch of song,
　　A song that all-too well we knew;
But whither had flown the ancient wrong;
　　And was it really I and you?
O since the end of life's to live
　　And pay in pence the common debt,
What should it cost us to forgive
　　Whose daily task is to forget?

You babbled in the well-known voice—
　　Not new, not new, the words you said.
You touched me off that famous poise,
　　That old effect, of neck and head.

Dear, was it really you and I ?
In truth the riddle 's ill to read,
So many are the deaths we die
Before we can be dead indeed.

## XVI

SPACE and dread and the dark—
Over a livid stretch of sky
Cloud-monsters crawling like a funeral
    train
Of huge primeval presences
Stooping beneath the weight
Of some enormous, rudimentary grief;
While in the haunting loneliness
The far sea waits and wanders with a
    sound
As of the trailing skirts of Destiny
Passing unseen

To some immitigable end
With her grey henchman, Death.


What larve, what spectre is this
Thrilling the wilderness to life
As with the bodily shape of Fear?
What but a desperate sense,
A strong foreboding of those dim,
Interminable continents, forlorn
And many-silenced in a dusk
Inviolable utterly and dead
As the poor dead it huddles and swarms and
    styes
In hugger-mugger through eternity?


Life—life—let there be life!
Better a thousand times the roaring hours
When wave and wind,

# RHYMES AND RHYTHMS

Like the Arch-Murderer in flight
From the Avenger at his heel,
Storm through the desolate fastnesses
And wild waste places of the world!

Life—give me life until the end,
That at the very top of being,
The battle-spirit shouting in my blood,
Out of the reddest hell of the fight
I may be snatched and flung
Into the everlasting lull,
The immortal, incommunicable dream.

## XVII

## *CARMEN PATIBULARE*

## (To H. S.)

Tree, Old Tree of the Triple Crook
  And the rope of the Black Election,
'Tis the faith of the Fool that a race you rule
  Can never achieve perfection :
So 'It's O for the time of the new Sublime
  And the better than human way
When the Wolf (poor beast) shall come to his
    own
  And the Rat shall have his day !'

For Tree, Old Tree of the Triple Beam
  And the power of provocation,

You have cockered the Brute with your dreadful
fruit
Till your thought is mere stupration:
And 'It's how should we rise to be pure and wise,
And how can we choose but fall,
So long as the Hangman makes us dread
And the Noose floats free for all?'


So Tree, Old Tree of the Triple Coign
And the trick there's no recalling,
They will haggle and hew till they hack you
through
And at last they lay you sprawling:
When 'Hey! for the hour of the race in flower
And the long good-bye to sin!'
And 'Ho! for the fires of Hell gone out
For the want of keeping in!'

But Tree, Old Tree of the Triple Bough
 And the ghastly Dreams that tend you,
Your growth began with the life of Man
 And only his death can end you :
They may tug in line at your hempen twine,
 They may flourish with axe and saw,
But your taproot drinks of the Sacred Springs
 In the living rock of Law.

And Tree, Old Tree of the Triple Fork,
 When the spent sun reels and blunders
Down a welkin lit with the flare of the Pit
 As it seethes in spate and thunders,
Stern on the glare of the tortured air
 Your lines august shall gloom,
And your master-beam be the last thing whelmed
 In the ruining roar of Doom.

XVIII

(To M. E. H.)

WHEN you wake in your crib,
You, an inch of experience—
Vaulted about
With the wonder of darkness;
Wailing and striving
To reach from your feebleness
Something you feel
Will be good to and cherish you,
Something you know
And can rest upon blindly:
O then a hand
(Your mother's, your mother's!)
By the fall of its fingers

All knowledge, all power to you,
Out of the dreary,
Discouraging strangenesses
Comes to and masters you,
Takes you, and lovingly
Woos you and soothes you
Back, as you cling to it,
Back to some comforting
Corner of sleep.


So you wake in your bed,
Having lived, having loved :
But the shadows are there,
And the world and its kingdoms
Incredibly faded ;
And you grope through the Terror
Above you and under
For the light, for the warmth,

The assurance of life;
But the blasts are ice-born,
And your heart is nigh burst
With the weight of the gloom
And the stress of your strangled
And desperate endeavour:
Sudden a hand—
Mother, O Mother!—
God at His best to you,
Out of the roaring,
Impossible silences,
Falls on and urges you,
Mightily, tenderly,
Forth, as you clutch at it,
Forth to the infinite
Peace of the Grave.

## XIX

O Time and Change, they range and range
    From sunshine round to thunder !—
They glance and go as the great winds blow,
    And the best of our dreams drive under :
For Time and Change estrange, estrange—
    And, now they have looked and seen us,
O we that were dear we are all-too near
    With the thick of the world between us.

O Death and Time, they chime and chime
    Like bells at sunset falling !—
They end the song, they right the wrong,
    They set the old echoes calling.:

For Death and Time bring on the prime
  Of God's own chosen weather,
And we lie in the peace of the Great Release
  As once in the grass together.

## XX

THE shadow of Dawn ;
Stillness and stars and over-mastering dreams
Of Life and Death and Sleep ;
Heard over gleaming flats the old unchanging
    sound
Of the old unchanging Sea.

My soul and yours—
O hand in hand let us fare forth, two ghosts,
Into the ghostliness,
The infinite and abounding solitudes,
Beyond—O beyond !—beyond . . .

# RHYMES AND RHYTHMS

Here in the porch

Upon the multitudinous silences

Of the kingdoms of the grave,

We twain are you and I—two ghosts Omnipotence

Can touch no more . . . no more!

## XXI

When the wind storms by with a shout, and the
stern sea-caves

Exult in the tramp and the roar of onsetting
waves,

Then, then, it comes home to the heart that the
top of life

Is the passion that burns the blood in the act of
strife—

Till you pity the dead down there in their quiet
graves.

But to drowse with the fen behind and the fog
before,

When the rain-rot spreads and a tame sea mumbles
the shore,

Not to adventure, none to fight, no right and no
wrong,

Sons of the Sword heart-sick for a stave of your
sire's old song—

O you envy the blessèd dead that can live no
more !

# RHYMES AND RHYTHMS

## XXII

Trees and the menace of night ;
Then a long, lonely, leaden mere
Backed by a desolate fell
As by a spectral battlement ; and then,
Low-brooding, interpenetrating all,
A vast, grey, listless, inexpressive sky,
So beggared, so incredibly bereft
Of starlight and the song of racing worlds
It might have bellied down upon the Void
Where as in terror Light was beginning to be.

Hist !   In the trees fulfilled of night
(Night and the wretchedness of the sky)

Is it the hurry of the rain?
Or the noise of a drive of the Dead
Streaming before the irresistible Will
Through the strange dusk of this, the
    Debateable Land
Between their place and ours?

Like the forgetfulness
Of the work-a-day world made visible,
A mist falls from the melancholy sky:
A messenger from some lost and loving
    soul,
Hopeless, far wandered, dazed
Here in the provinces of life,
A great white moth fades miserably past.

Thro' the trees in the strange dead night,
Under the vast dead sky,

Forgetting and forgot, a drift of Dead

Sets to the mystic mere, the phantom
   fell,

And the unimagined vastitudes beyond.

## XXIII

### (To P. A. G.)

HERE they trysted, here they strayed
  In the leafage dewy and boon,
Many a man and many a maid,
  And the morn was merry June :
'Death is fleet, Life is sweet,'
  Sang the blackbird in the may ;
And the hour with flying feet
  While they dreamed was yesterday.

Many a maid and many a man
  Found the leafage close and boon ;
Many a destiny began—
  O the morn was merry June.

118

Dead and gone, dead and gone,
  (Hark the blackbird in the may !),
Life and Death went hurrying on,
  Cheek on cheek—and where were they ?

Dust in dust engendering dust
  In the leafage fresh and boon,
Man and maid fulfil their trust—
  Still the morn turns merry June.
Mother Life, Father Death
  (O the blackbird in the may !),
Each the other's breath for breath,
  Fleet the times of the world away.

## XXIV

## (To A. C.)

Not to the staring Day,
For all the importunate questionings he pursues
In his big, violent voice,
Shall those mild things of bulk and multitude,
God's foresters, the Trees,
Yield of their huge unutterable selves.
Midsummer-manifold, each one
Voluminous, a labyrinth of life,
They keep their greenest musings and the dim
    dreams
That haunt their leafier privacies

Dissembled, baffling the random gapeseed still
With blank full-faces or the innocent guile
Of laughter flickering back from shine to shade,
And disappearances of homing birds,
And frolicsome freaks
Of little boughs that frisk with little boughs.


But at the word
Of the ancient, sacerdotal Night,
Night of the many secrets, whose effect—
Transfiguring, hierophantic, dread—
Themselves alone may fully apprehend,
They tremble and are changed :
In each, the uncouth individual soul
Looms forth and glooms
Essential, and, their bodily presences
Touched with inordinate significance,
Wearing the darkness like the livery

Of some mysterious and tremendous guild,
They brood—they menace—they appal:
Or the anguish of prophecy tears them, and they
      wring
Wild hands of warning in the face
Of some inevitable advance of doom:
Or, each to the other bending, beckoning, signing,
As in some monstrous market-place,
They pass the news, these Gossips of the Prime,
In that old speech their forefathers
Learned on the lawns of Eden, ere they heard
The troubled voice of Eve
Naming the wondering folk of Paradise.


Your sense is sealed, or you should hear them tell
The tale of their dim life and all
Its compost of experience: how the Sun

Spreads them their daily feast,

Sumptuous, of light, firing them as with wine;

Of the old Moon's fitful solicitude

And those mild messages the Stars

Descend in silver silences and dews;

Or what the sweet-breathing West,

Wanton with wading in the swirl of the wheat,

Said, and their leafage laughed;

And how the wet-winged Angel of the Rain

Came whispering . . . whispering; and the gifts
    of the Year—

The sting of the stirring sap

Under the wizardry of the young-eyed Spring,

Their summer amplitudes of pomp

And rich autumnal melancholy, and the shrill,

Embittered housewifery

Of the lean Winter: all such things,

And with them all the goodness of the Master

Whose right hand blesses with increase and
    life,
Whose left hand honours with decay and death.


Thus under the constraint of Night
These gross and simple creatures,
Each in his scores of rings, which rings are years,
A servant of the Will.
And God, the Craftsman, as He walks
The floor of His workshop, hearkens, full of cheer
In thus accomplishing
The aims of His miraculous artistry.

## XXV

WHAT have I done for you,
   England, my England?
What is there I would not do,
   England, my own?
With your glorious eyes austere,
As the Lord were walking near,
Whispering terrible things and dear
   As the Song on your bugles blown,
     England—
Round the world on your bugles blown!

Where shall the watchful Sun,
   England, my England,
Match the master-work you've done,
   England, my own?

125

When shall he rejoice agen

Such a breed of mighty men

As come forward, one to ten,

    To the Song on your bugles blown,

        England—

    Down the years on your bugles blown?


Ever the faith endures,

    England, my England :—

'Take and break us : we are yours,

    'England, my own !

'Life is good, and joy runs high

'Between English earth and sky :

'Death is death ; but we shall die

    'To the Song on your bugles blown,

        'England—

    'To the stars on your bugles blown !'

They call you proud and hard,
    England, my England :
You with worlds to watch and ward,
    England, my own !
You whose mailed hand keeps the keys
Of such teeming destinies
You could know nor dread nor ease
       Were the Song on your bugles blown,
          England,
       Round the Pit on your bugles blown !


Mother of Ships whose might,
    England, my England,
Is the fierce old Sea's delight,
    England, my own,
Chosen daughter of the Lord,
Spouse-in-Chief of the ancient Sword,

There's the menace of the Word
    In the Song on your bugles blown,
        England—
    Out of heaven on your bugles blown!

# EPILOGUE

*SOMETHING is dead . . .*

*The grace of sunset solitudes, the march*

*Of the solitary moon, the pomp and power*

*Of round on round of shining soldier-stars*

*Patrolling space, the bounties of the sun—*

*Sovran, tremendous, inaccessible—*

*The multitudinous friendliness of the sea,*

*Possess no more—no more.*


*Something is dead . . .*

*The autumn rain-rot deeper and wider soaks*

*And spreads, the burden of winter heavier weighs,*

# EPILOGUE

*His melancholy close and closer yet*
*Cleaves, and those incantations of the Spring*
*That made the heart a centre of miracles*
*Grow formal, and the wonder-working hours*
*Arise no more—no more.*

*Something is dead . . .*
*'Tis time to creep in close about the fire*
*And tell grey tales of what we were, and dream*
*Old dreams and faded, and as we may rejoice*
*In the young life that round us leaps and laughs,*
*A fountain in the sunshine, in the pride*
*Of God's best gift that to us twain returns,*
*Dear Heart, no more—no more.*

Edinburgh : T. and A. CONSTABLE
Printers to Her Majesty

WILLIAM ERNEST HENLEY

# VIEWS AND REVIEWS

## ESSAYS IN APPRECIATION

Second Edition.

*LITERATURE*

16mo.  XII.-235 pages.  Printed by CONSTABLE
Cloth, top gilt

### Price 5s. *nett.*

*\*\* Twenty Copies printed on Japanese vellum and bound
in half-morocco.  Four Copies remain for
sale at Two Guineas each*

The SPECTATOR.—'This is one of the most remarkable
volumes of literary criticism—in more senses than one it is the
most striking—that have appeared for a number of years.  Mr.
Henley has been known for a considerable time as one of the
most fearless, if not also as one of the most uncompromising, of
art critics, the sworn foe of conventionality in "paint" and of

K

flabby timidity in writing the truth about it. More recently he published a volume of poems, full of character, and in which " our lady of pain " figured as a reality of the writer's experience, not as a mere Swinburnian phantom. And now in this volume of *Views and Reviews* he figures as a prose critic in literature. . . . His book is not so much one of literary criticism, in the ordinary and proper sense of the word, as of brilliant table-talk. . . . Taken altogether, *Views and Reviews* will provoke as much censure as commendation, for whatever may be Mr. Henley's faults, a commonplace habit of looking at men and things is not one of them. He is a master of a most remarkable and attractive style,—sometimes, indeed, he seems to be the servant of it. His book, therefore, deserves to be read, and will be read. And yet, unless we are much mistaken, it is but its author's preliminary canter in the field of criticism.'

The NATIONAL OBSERVER.—' This book, in many respects brilliant, unsatisfactory in not a few, is remarkable in all. . . . It is but rarely that you fall in with so choice and desirable an example of the printer's craft. . . . The author's style, the author's point of view, above all the author's ever present personality, bind these fragments into a sufficiently perceptible and intelligible whole. . . . Mr. Henley's style is not equable nor serene, nor classic. Rather is it full of surprises, restless and capricious, with moments of immense power and dazzling brilliance.'

The SPEAKER.—'A good book of criticism. . . . Mr. Henley has much in common with modern French criticism. There is something of the same robustness of tone, magisterial finality of deliverance uncompromising utterance of personal conviction, something also of the same strong and close grip of his subject. ; . . . He claims for himself "an honest regard for letters"; we may concede to him also other good qualities—sincerity, knowledge, and strength. His judgments are in the main clear-sighted, sane, humane, and generous.'

The ATHENÆUM.—'The exceeding liveliness of his style, his fondness for epigram and antithesis, his love of paradox and generalisation, his faculty of adapting old phrases to new uses, and other characteristics of his, attract and delight the reader. . . . He possesses a wide range of reading, real insight, a hearty appreciation of good literature, and a genuine faculty of making just comparisons. A collection of brilliant yet thoughtful observations on authors and books in which there is not a dull line, and which contains much that is at once original and true.'

The ACADEMY (signed Oliver Elton).—'A rare and fine critical perception. . . . It is crammed with good things, and the good things are those of a man who can be both a wit and a poet.'

The BOOK GAZETTE.—'Mr. Henley is one of the most facile and charming writers of prose and verse in some of their guises that we possess. . . . The subjects he has preferred from all others in this volume are in themselves gems, and Mr. Henley has mounted them in a setting of his own design. This design is chaste and elegant, though, indeed, simple and free from ostentation.'

LIVRE MODERNE.—' Un petit livre qui intéressera beaucoup tous les Français qui sont familiers avec la langue anglaise.'

The GRAPHIC.—'A series of bright, witty, rapid characterisations of literary men, of the present and of the past of our own and other countries.'

The BRITISH WEEKLY (signed J. M. Barrie).—'Much wit, and here and there aphorisms that one may remember to be met before in newspapers, and wondered who made them. . . . Written in poet's English. . . . The printing (by the Constables) is a joy to the eye.'

The GUARDIAN.—'Good criticism, that keenest spur to the enjoyment of good literature, is none so common in this country that we can afford to pass over an addition to it in silence. . . . We cannot but acknowledge that he has put forth a real scheme, that he has tested the writers who have passed before him by real tests, that he has put results of candour and of true, though perhaps not very broad toleration, down in language which is for the most part at once dexterous and definite, at once critical and picturesque, at once sober and yet full of colour.'

The CHURCH REFORMER.—'A more valuable contribution to literary criticism has not been given to the public for many years. . . . The strength, boldness, and honesty of his judgments are beyond all praise.'

The TABLET.—'The book has something of the inimitable. There is force, there is selection, there is simplicity without blankness and elaboration without cramp. There is felicity everywhere, and a cleverness which is welcomed the more keenly for its rare companion, an abiding respect for the language in which it barters. . . . Throughout, moreover, there is the distinction which Mr. Coventry Patmore has denied as the attribute of any writer new in the last twenty years ; that distinction which being of the aristocracy of letters is in-describable (even by epigram), and is yet very secure.'

The CHRISTIAN LEADER characterises the volume as 'sparkling,' and PEARSON'S WEEKLY as 'charming,' while THE STAR condemns it as ' much overrated.'

The ST. JAMES'S GAZETTE.—' Doubly welcome. It is good in itself, and seems even better than it is by comparison with so much that is either positively or negatively bad. He has some-thing to say about forty authors, from Theocritus to Mr. Austin Dobson, and from Shakespeare to Dickens and Thackeray. He has read widely and well, he has thought for himself, he has the courage of his opinions, and he has a genuine love for all that is best and worthiest in literature. . . . *Views and Reviews* is a book to be viewed and reviewed by the real lover of literature, not once only, but again and again.'

The SCOTSMAN.—' The pieces are homogeneous with one another, mainly because of the sincerity of Mr. Henley's judg-ments on literature. . . . They are always earnest and honest, which is as much as to say that they are always interesting. . . . Not only readable from beginning to end (as is rare in a book of collected criticisms), but stimulating and suggestive in no common degree.'

The GLASGOW HERALD.—'If Mr. Henley can be said to belong to any school in literature, it is to the school of reaction in favour of virility and action against namby-pambyism, sentimentality and introspection. . . . Of this school Mr. Henley is out of sight the best all-round stylist.'

The NORTH BRITISH DAILY MAIL.—'Mr. Henley has constructed a work well qualified by its intrinsic merits to take a high place in the world of pure literature. The essays are a delight to read, and they furnish a curriculum through which all students of letters, old and young, may pass with profit.'

The SCOTTISH LEADER.—'His prose technique presents much of the merit, one may say the genius, of his verse; it has vividness, freshness, concision, boldness, and felicity in epithet.'

The LIVERPOOL DAILY POST.—'The author of these essays claims for himself "an honest regard for letters." He has more than this, being very much of a literary specialist. . . . His utterances are characterised by a directness and a sureness that are quite French in tone, and with him, as with the French critics, the personal conviction is not unpleasantly obtruded.'

The NORTH METROPOLITAN PRESS.—'He who cares for opinions, vigorous and heroic, set forth in a style at once brilliant and convincing, must not miss *Views and Reviews.*'

The GLASGOW EVENING CITIZEN.—'The author has a fluent and epigrammatic mode of expressing himself which makes his book very readable.'

The PERTHSHIRE ADVERTISER.—'Has no equal for brilliancy of style, condensed genius of expression, and literary grasp.'

The AUSTRALASIAN.—' Exception may be taken to some of Mr. Henley's judgments, but one is struck by their general fairness, honesty and sincerity. Moreover, his literary style possesses a certain piquancy and point which are decidedly attractive.'

The MELBOURNE ARGUS.—' Bright, sparkling, and pointed, in very good, clear, simple English.'

The EUROPEAN MAIL.—' Be his subject what it may, there is a purity of artistic purpose pervading the whole. . . . His readers will find that what he offers them from his stores is deficient neither in savour nor in substance.'

The COLONIES AND INDIA.—' A guide to common-sense in the way of criticism ; and not only to common-sense, but to style, to versatility of observation, and to truth in the dissection of mental qualities.'

The NEW YORK TRIBUNE.—' Original, keen, and felicitous. . . . Delicate and discriminating literary taste, and a happy faculty for analysis and comparison.'

The PHILADELPHIA LEDGER.—' He interfuses his criticism with the thought, the expressions, the personal glow of the author he is discussing.'

The BOSTON TIMES.—' Keen analysis, clever characterisation, and delightful expression.'

The CHICAGO TIMES.—' Thoughtful, vigorous, and stimulative.'

The SAN FRANCISCO CHRONICLE.—' No more keen and pungent criticism has been printed in these days.'

WILLIAM ERNEST HENLEY

# A BOOK OF VERSES

## IN HOSPITAL: RHYMES AND RHYTHMS.
## LIFE AND DEATH (ECHOES).
## BRIC-À-BRAC: BALLADS, RONDELS,
## SONNETS, QUATORZAINS,
## AND RONDEAUS.

Fourth Edition.

16mo.  Cloth,

*with Etched Title-page Vignette of the Old Infirmary,
Edinburgh,* by W. HOLE, A.R.S.A.

Price 5*s*.

The SPECTATOR says 'the author is a genuine poet . . .
there is freshness in all he writes, and music in much of it, and,
what is perhaps rarer, a clear eye for outline and colour, and
character in a good deal of it. . . . Mr. Henley's keenness of
vision, freshness of feeling, and capacity for song are unmis-
takeable.'

For the SATURDAY REVIEW 'the ring of genuine and virile humanity is more singular in this volume than its clever workmanship.' It further commends 'his lusty vigour, his spirited ring, his touch of wholesome plainness and freshness.'

The ATHENÆUM discusses at length his 'realism, that is something more than pre-Raphaelite,' and notes his 'fine and winning kind of Rabelaisian heartiness,' and his 'manly and heroic expression of the temper of the sufferer.'

The UNIVERSAL REVIEW.—'It is *poetry*, not merely measured prose or successfully jangled verse. . . . Neither the fancy nor the melody of the verse forms the charm of the book, though there is enough of both to make the fortune of many a minor poet. The real excellence rather consists in the kindly philosophy, strong, yet tender withal, which breathes from these pages—the words of a man who has seen both the gaiety and the suffering of life, who has had his share in each, and who now looks tolerantly or bravely at happiness or pain.'

The ACADEMY.—' Mr. Henley's treatment of the Hospital theme . . . is powerful, genuine, and manly throughout. . . . Through the Dantesque world of his infirmary the joy of a strong life runs ever like a stream. . . . Most of the poems in the Life and Death section are love-songs, warm and throbbing from the heart.'

The ST. JAMES'S GAZETTE describes the volume as 'wholesome phantasy, wholesome feeling, wholesome human affection, expressed in adequate form. . . . The Hospital section is the literary picture of a section of human suffering which has not before found its artist. There is here the result of a direct experience by one who knows what to say, what to indicate, what to leave unsaid.'

The CRITIC (New York) thinks ' Mr. Henley the easy achiever of all he essays to do,' and signals out especially the 'jocosery, the grotesquery, and daintiness of form' of the BRIC-À-BRAC section.

The SCOTSMAN says 'the collection is one over which the lover of poetry will linger . . . for its natural simplicity and directness of feeling, its careful, choice, and harmonious handling of language.'

The WEEKLY REGISTER says of the Hospital poems, 'they may be painful sometimes, but there is a tenderness in them which is educative to the most fastidious.'

The SCOTTISH LEADER bolds the book 'to combine that realism of actual and detailed description with that obscure essence of feeling, held captive by the right words, which is the eternal distinction between prose and poetry. . . . Curiously and memorably vivid, full of deft phrasing, and perfectly free from prosaism.'

The GLASGOW HERALD notes the ' terse and vivid suggestion of landscape and natural features . . . the dignity and beauty of the Rondeaus.'

The SCOTS MAGAZINE commends the 'felicitous union of vigorous thinking with artistic deftness . . . the robust and spirited tone, the purity and grace of diction.'

‵ MERRY ENGLAND remarks that ‘ Mr. Henley, before writing his verses, has made a great sweeping movement, which has cleared out of his way all the methods and manners surrounding the practice of poetry—not merely the weak and large old traditions ostentatiously set aside by Wordsworth, but all the smaller conventionalities that are so constantly and imperceptibly accumulating. . . . A poem which, as usual with Mr. Henley, tells the truth, and tells it with vital sincerity.'

The MANCHESTER GUARDIAN observes : ‘ In a not inconsiderable reading of contemporary verse the two difficulties which we have observed as chiefly besetting the poet are—first, the difficulty of being forcible without being extravagant or grotesque, original without being far-fetched ; and, secondly, the difficulty of feeling and showing the restraint and discipline of literary sense and form without being mannered, bloodless, and unreal. Mr. Henley appears to us to have mastered both these in a very uncommon degree.'

Finally, the PALL MALL GAZETTE is of opinion that this ‘ is a horrible, fascinating, and wrong, yet rightly done, little book—a book which no one should be advised to read, and which no one would be content to have missed.'

LONDON

PUBLISHED BY DAVID NUTT

IN the STRAND

1893

WILLIAM ERNEST HENLEY

# LYRA HEROICA

AN ANTHOLOGY SELECTED FROM THE BEST

ENGLISH VERSE OF THE SIXTEENTH,

SEVENTEENTH, EIGHTEENTH, AND

NINETEENTH CENTURIES.

Library (Third) Edition.
Crown 8vo. XVIII+362 pp. cloth, uncut edges,
Stamped cover, 3*s*. 6*d*. ; or, School (Second) Edition,
12mo, cloth, 2*s*.

The ANTI-JACOBIN.—' It is a body of poetry in which every-
thing that goes to make up human life is exhibited in a spacious, lofty, noble, and therefore essentially heroic light. Its
ditties of "the camp, the court, the grove,"—its songs of love
and war, of sorrow and gladness, of passion and devotion, of
country and religion, one and all are the product of a muse
that "nothing common does or mean," but that dwells habitu-
ally in presence of the larger aspects and issues of things. Mr.
Henley modestly christens his volume "A Book of Verse for
Boys" ; and, although there is nothing puerile about it, by all
means let boys read it, for it is the kind of reading which will
help to make them men.'

˙ The SPECTATOR, November 21, 1891.—'No higher aim could well be than that which Mr. Henley has put before himself. His own words will best express it:—'' To set forth, as only art can, the beauty and the joy of living, the beauty and the blessedness of death, the glory of battle and adventure, the nobility of devotion—to a cause, an ideal, a passion even—the dignity of resistance, the sacred quality of patriotism, that is my ambition here." His selection is, on the whole, as good as can be.'

The WORLD, November 25, 1891.—'When we had picked all the holes we could in Mr. Henley's anthology, there would still be enough left to stir all the boys' hearts in the kingdom as by trumpet.'

The GUARDIAN, November 18, 1891.—'Mr. Henley's book, if not without predecessors, is very markedly distinguished from them. In part this distinction is one of form. The author's dedication runs, ''To Walter Blaikie, artist, printer, my part in this book," and if Mr. Blaikie is a member of the firm of T. & A. Constable, the printers of the book, and has superintended the production of the volume, he certainly has deserved Mr. Henley's gratitude. Print, paper, and arrangement are all beautiful, and the book is the lightest in proportion to its size which we have ever handled from any modern press. All this we note with real pleasure, and yet it sinks into insignificance beside the fact that Mr. Henley has brought to the task of selection an instinct alike for poetry and for chivalry which seems to us quite wonderfully, and even unerringly, right. There is not a poem in the volume which sinks below the level of true poetry considered as a work of art, and there is not a poem which does not breathe something of the spirit of that fine verse of Scott's which Mr. Henley has taken as his motto.'

The SATURDAY REVIEW, November 7, 1891.—'A very fine book, which will, we hope, help to keep the blood of many English boys from the wretched and morbid stagnation of modernity.'

The SCOTTISH LEADER.—'The ideal gift-book of the year.'

The NATIONAL OBSERVER.—'On the whole the most representative and the most inspiring anthology with which we are acquainted.'

The GLASGOW HERALD.—'Mr. Henley has done his work admirably—we may even say perfectly.'

The STAR, October 29, 1891.—'This perfectly lovely volume. Though Mr. Henley's selection is but another proof of his love for battle (as of the Scriptural war-horse that crieth "Ha! Ha!" among the javelins), it is proof also that he loves good poetry no less.'

The DUBLIN EVENING MAIL.—'Edited with admirable critical judgment and conscientious care.'

The DAILY GRAPHIC.—'A selection which all boys should and most boys will appreciate.'

The BRITISH WEEKLY, November 19, 1891.—'A collection of the noblest verse in our language that has value for theme, and beginning with Shakespeare, it does not leave off until it has sampled Mr. Kipling. *Lyra Heroica* is a rare good book; there is nothing else of the kind in our language; and the boy who has to wait more than three calendar months for it ought to tell them at the local bookshop to put it down to his father's account.'

LOUISE CHANDLER MOULTON, in the *Boston U.S.A. Herald* of Sunday, November 15.—'One of the best anthologies by which literature has ever been enriched.'

The EDUCATIONAL REVIEW.—'This book should be looked at by all who wish to make a handsome present to a boy; they will be persuaded to choose it.'

The SCOTSMAN.—'Never was a better book of the kind put together.'

The LEEDS MERCURY.—'The book is one which all lovers of poetry will appreciate.'

The PALL MALL GAZETTE.—'Mr. Henley has done the work as well as anybody else could have done it, and perhaps better than most. . . . Every boy ought to have this book, and most men.'

The MANCHESTER GUARDIAN.—'New anthologies are almost the most delightful of new books to cut and, in an irresponsible fashion, to criticise. It is delightful to find one's favourite lyrics valued as one would have them ; delightful also to find the reverse, and to feel indignantly sure that one respectable man of letters at least has shown less taste than we. In looking through Mr. Henley's *Lyra Heroica*, the former delight is felt more than the latter, and that is the highest praise that a critic made of flesh and blood and human dislikes and likings can give to a new collection of the kind.'

The EDINBURGH MEDICAL JOURNAL.—'He has mixed songs of battle, of love, constancy, and patriotism so well that even those who are boys no longer may be stirred and heartened.'

The ILLUSTRATED LONDON NEWS.—'Worthy to be placed on the same shelf as our "Golden Treasuries." . . . Though admirably adapted to stimulate courage and patriotism in the young, it will be equally welcome to the adult.'

The SPEAKER.—'Mr. Henley's is a very fine ambition, and it will hardly be denied that his is a splendid book of verse.'

The NORTH BRITISH DAILY MAIL.—'May be commended unreservedly.'

The TABLET.—'Take it all in all, as a present for boys, and for men for that matter, *Lyra Heroica*, printed with perfection and handsomely bound, is a book among books, an anthology among anthologies.'

The ST. JAMES'S GAZETTE.—'In the eyes of that curious Radical section to whom all war, for whatever purpose, on behalf of whatever principle, is a crime, this book must seem the most dangerous and most immoral that was ever put into the hands of youth ; for it sings the glory of noble and honourable war. Its note is a note of healthy and resolute defiance —the defiance of liberty to bondage, of duty to disgrace, of courage to misfortune.'

The CRITIC (New York), December 5, 1891.—'Selected with the taste and judgment of a poet.'

The NORTHERN DAILY NEWS, December 18, 1891.—'Mr. Henley's taste is robust and catholic, and offers a welcome to many spirited lyrics that are not generally considered classical.'

The GRAPHIC, December 26, 1891.—'By far the best of the books of verse for boys. . . . The judgment shown throughout in selection and editing is excellent. The volume should be in the hands of every English boy.'

The NATIONAL REVIEW.—'A manly book, which should delight manly boys and manly men as well.'

The IRISH DAILY INDEPENDENT, January 4, 1892.—'Mr. Henley's *Lyra Heroica* is like the blast of a trumpet, and it would be hard indeed to make a milksop of a lad nourished on these noble numbers.

L

SYLVIA'S JOURNAL, March 1892.—'Beyond comparison the noblest anthology of stirring poems and ballads in the English language—probably in any language. . . . A more nobly planned and excellently carried out volume it were hard to name. Paper, binding, and print (the last a triumph of the printer's art) are all that could be wished. If any of my readers have brothers to whom they wish to give a book, let me advise them to get *Lyra Heroica*. If the brothers do not like it (though I go bail they will), the volume is one which any English maiden will be glad enough to have upon her shelf.'

LONDON

PUBLISHED BY D A V I D  N U T T

IN the STRAND

1893